HAPPY FAMILY

HAPPY FAMILY

POEMS BY

JANE SHORE

Picador USA
New York

Picador® is a U.S. registered trademark and is used by
St. Martin's Press under license from Pan Books Limited.

For information on Picador USA Reading Group Guides,
as well as ordering, please contact the Trade Marketing
department at St. Martin's Press.
Phone: 1-800-221-7945 extension 763
Fax: 212-677-7456
E-mail: trademarketing@stmartins.com

Production Editor: David Stanford Burr

Library of Congress Cataloging-in-Publication Data

Shore, Jane.
    Happy family : poems / Jane Shore.
       p.   cm.
    ISBN 0-312-20310-1 (hc)
    ISBN 0-312-26334-1 (pbk)
    1. Women Poetry. I. Title.
  PS3569.H5795H3 1999
  811'.54—dc21   99-29860
                                                CIP

First Picador USA Paperback Edition: October 2000

10 9 8 7 6 5 4 3 2 1

ACKNOWLEDGMENTS

My thanks to the editors of the following journals and anthologies, where these poems first appeared (some in earlier versions):

"Happiness" in *Contemporary American Poetry: A Bread Loaf Anthology*, edited by Michael Collier and Stanley Plumly.

"Sawdust" in *Poems for a Small Planet, A Bread Loaf Anthology*, edited by Robert Pack and Jay Parini.

"Fairbanks Museum and Planetarium" in *The George Washington Magazine*.

"Fairbanks Museum and Planetarium" and "Public Service Is Rich Enough" in *A New England Anthology*, edited by Robert Pack and Jay Parini.

"The Uncanny" and "Reprise" in *Pequod*.

"Mrs. Hitler" and "Shit Soup" in *Salmagundi*.

"Small Talk" in TriQuarterly.

and to Lorrie Goldensohn, Jody Bolz, Barry Goldensohn, Chana Bloch, Joyce Johnson, Gregory Orr, Julie Agoos, Ellen Voigt, and Anne Caston.

For Howard and Emma,
and Florence Abramowitz

CONTENTS

ONE

TWO

... All of them are gone
Except for me; and for me nothing is gone—

—Randall Jarrell
"Thinking of the Lost World"

ONE

HAPPY FAMILY

In Chinatown, we order Happy Family,
the Specialty of the House.
The table set; red paper placemats
inscribed with the Chinese zodiac.
My husband's an ox; my daughter's
a dragon, hungry and cranky; I'm a pig.
The stars will tell us whether
we at this table are compatible.

The waiter vanishes into the kitchen.
Tea steeps in the metal teapot.
My husband plays with his napkin.
In the booth behind him sits a couple
necking, apparently in love.

Every Saturday night after work,
my mother ordered takeout from the Hong Kong,
the only Chinese restaurant in town.
She filled the teakettle.
By the time it boiled,
the table was set, minus knives and forks,
and my father had fetched the big brown paper bag
leaking grease: five shiny white
food cartons stacked inside.

My little sister and I unpacked the food,
unsheathed the wooden chopsticks—
Siamese twins joined at the shoulders—
which we snapped apart.
Thirteen years old, moody, brooding,

daydreaming about boys,
I sat and ate safe chop suey,
bland Cantonese shrimp,
moo goo gai pan, and egg foo yung.

My mother somber, my father drained,
too exhausted from work to talk,
as if the clicking chopsticks
were knitting something in their mouths.
My mother put hers aside
and picked at her shrimp with a fork.
She dunked a Lipton teabag in her cup
until the hot water turned rusty,
refusing the Hong Kong's complimentary tea,
no brand she'd ever seen before.

I cleared the table,
put empty cartons back in the bag.
Glued to the bottom,
translucent with oil, the pale green bill
a maze of Chinese characters.
Between the sealed lips of my fortune cookie,
a white scrap of tongue poking out . . .

Tonight, the waiter brings Happy Family
steaming under a metal dome
and three small igloos of rice.
Mounded on the white oval plate, the unlikely
marriage of meat and fish, crab and chicken.
Not all Happy Families are alike.
The chef's tossed in wilted greens

and water chestnuts, silk against crunch;
he's added fresh ginger to baby corn,
carrots, bamboo shoots, scallions, celery,
broccoli, pea pods, bok choy.
My daughter impales a chunk of beef
on her chopstick and contentedly
sucks on it, like a popsicle.
Eating Happy Family, we all begin to smile.

I prod the only thing left on the plate,
a large garnish
carved in the shape of an open rose.
Is it a turnip? An Asian pear?
The edges of the delicate petals
tinged with pink dye, the flesh
white and cool as a peeled apple's.
My daughter reaches for it—

"No good to eat!" The waiter rushes over—
"Rutabaga! Not cooked! Poison!"—

and hands us a plate with the bill
buried under three fortune cookies—
our teeth already tearing
at the cellophane, our fingers prying open
our three fates.

BUYING A STAR

An ad on the radio says that you can buy a star.
Call the toll-free number, charge it
to your credit card, and they'll send you
a parchment certificate of authenticity
and constellation chart with your actual star circled,
mapping your province of gaseous darkness, fire and ice,
over which you can rule, like the Creator.
The summer we got married, remember the night
we wrapped ourselves in blankets
and lay on our backs on the hood of our Toyota,
watching the meteor shower?
For an hour, we lay so still—
a husband and wife side by side
atop the stone lid of a medieval sarcophagus.
Beneath us, the damp grass
shivered with crickets and, above,
quick as eye blinks,
meteors streaked across the sky.
Every few seconds we'd see one die.
There! there! in the upper-right-hand corner—
no mortgage, no upkeep, no perpetual care—
there we are! buried in darkness, flashing,
then *out.*

For Howard

SCIENCE FAIR

"You might think the Earth
is going to be here forever,"
my third-grade teacher said,
but one day the sun will burn itself out.
It will happen about five billion years from now,
but by then you and everybody here
will be dead."

She seemed surprised at her own words.

Our class walked single file to the gym,
past dissected frogs,
sparking electric wires,
magnets that attracted and repelled.
We played volleyball
under a model of the solar system
suspended from a ceiling beam.

Three o'clock, after school let out,
I hung around my family's dress shop.
At six, my father switched on the alarm;
we went to our apartment upstairs.
By nine, my bedtime,
every store on my block was dark;
on either side of us—
the butcher shop and the bakery—
rooms in a locked museum.

I lay awake.
In the bakery's big glass case,
the dummy birthday cakes
were on display, icing hard as stucco.
On top of one, a ballerina's pointed toe
stuck in an iced rosette,
her raised, extended leg
like a sundial's gnomon casting its shadow.

Tacked to the wall
behind the butcher's chopping block,
a chart showed the cuts of meat—
a cow mapped out like the 48 States—
the animal put away for the night
inside a refrigerator big as a bank vault.

At two in the morning,
a dream woke me—
seven balls dangled on strings:
Mercury painted red, Venus green,
a blue Earth circled the light-bulb sun
flickering on and off,
a blue ribbon pinned underneath a sign:
THE SUN AND ITS FAMILY OF PLANETS.

Every time I closed my eyes,
the bulb flickered, and I saw
the Earth's blue tempera crust
flaking and peeling, the pink rubber ball
underneath it showing through.

One day it will all be gone.
The Earth, and all the people on it.

I couldn't fall asleep again.
I threw off my blanket, I tried moving
to the other side of my bed.
To calm myself, I recited the names
of the stores on my block:

Phil's Parkside Liquors, Delancy's Candy,
Ernie's Upholstery, Wolf's Deli,
Nick's One Hour Martinizing, Tony's Shoe Repair,
and *The Rolling Pin Bake Shop,* next door,
Corduroy Village—my father's store—
and *Noveck's Drugs,* on the corner—

over and over, until I climbed the stairs, home.

THE SECOND COMING

Rabbi Nissenbaum was the substitute
the day our Hebrew teacher had the flu.
He sat on Mr. Frank's desk, dressed
for business in black suit and shoes,
glasses, mustache, and yarmulke.
On the blackboard behind him,
dusty clouds of *chais*
dissolved in the swirling firmament
over which the rabbi pulled down,
like a window shade,
a map of the Holy Land
rolled up and down so often
its deserts had wrinkles instead of dunes.

The rabbi spoke plain English,
unlike Mr. Frank, whom our temple
had recruited from Israel.
Balding, pale, unmarried, unhappy,
Mr. Frank spoke in a thick accent
we imitated behind his back.
The rabbi, on the other hand,
was American, like us.
He was onto our tricks.

The rabbi's wooden yardstick rapped
at ancient Palestine, and at its neighbor,
Egypt, where a few thirsty camels,
bigger than the pyramids,
stood beside the long blue
varicose vein of the Nile.
Babylonians and Jews.
Egyptians and Jews.
Philistines and Jews.

I was twelve. Old enough to see
Israelis fighting Arabs
every night on the evening news.

Then the rabbi pulled down
a modern map over the old one.
Saudi Arabia. Iran. Egypt.
Israel looked so small
next to those Goliaths.
Oil rigs like little Eiffel Towers
dotted the deserts near the Red Sea
and the Dead Sea, and the red
gash of the Suez Canal.

The rabbi cleared his throat.
"Class," he coughed, "I'm here today
to answer questions."
A row behind me, Tina and Marty
were playing footsie under a desk.
Steve Usden doodled on his arm.
I raised my hand. Someone had to.
Steve gave me a dirty look.
"Rabbi," I said, "Jesus started out Jewish.
Then he started a religion of his own.
If Jesus was Jewish,
how come *we* don't worship him?"

My family worshipped everyone else
who was Jewish.
Eight o'clock every Sunday night,
we'd sit in our living room
and watch Ed Sullivan on television,
my aunts and uncles clapping at the screen
whenever a Jew came on.

Richard Tucker? *A great Jewish tenor.*
A cantor, who made it big in opera.
Jack Benny? *A great Jewish comedian.*
A penny-pincher, he made millions.
Sammy Davis Jr.? *A great entertainer.*
A shvartzer, but he converted,
so now he's a Jew, too.

The rabbi wet his lips.
Out from a pocket came a handkerchief.
"Boys and girls," he said, "we believe
that when the true Messiah comes—
the *Mashiach,* the anointed one—
there will be peace on Earth.
How could Jesus be the Messiah
when there are still wars,
people killing each other,
sickness, suffering, and famine?"
Rabbi Nissenbaum looked grim.
"That's why we don't believe in Him.
Any other questions?"

Pipes knocked overhead.
I raised my hand. Again.
"Rabbi, *when* will the Messiah come?"

The rabbi removed his glasses
and wiped them with the handkerchief.
Under the bright fluorescent lights
his cheeks were beginning to darken
with five o'clock shadow.
He lowered his voice.
"The Messiah will come
when oil once more flows upon the land."

I didn't understand.
Was that Rabbi Nissenbaum talking?
Or a prophet from the Bible?
It wasn't his usual, matter-of-fact style.

The rabbi yawned. On the map
behind him, the Dead Sea came alive
like water boiling in a pan:
I glanced at the Jordan River,
but instead of water,
oil spilled over the banks,
oil bubbled up from the desert floor,
in geysers, like Old Faithful,
a giant tidal wave of oil
anointed every grain of sand,
choking the stones of the Wailing Wall
and swallowing Jerusalem.

The rabbi folded his handkerchief
and stuffed it back into his pants.
He scratched under his yarmulke.
The classroom became as still
as before the world was made.
"Jane, dear," he sighed,
glancing at the ceiling,
"we'll know the Messiah has come
when the lion lies down with the lamb."

For Tova Reich and R. D. Eno

GOD

Mary, my baby-sitter, once took me on a bus
to her shabby boardinghouse in Jersey City
where she showed me a white plastic statue
of a bearded man wearing a bathrobe
who stood on her dresser among her dime-store perfumes.
I remember Mary telling me, "This is God."

God was about the size of a bottle
of eau de cologne, light as a chicken bone.
I held Him in one hand, turning Him over,
the way you'd examine an object
you'd picked up off the ground, thinking it was
just a rock but a minute later discovering
it was a gold ring, and how lucky you were
finding a thing like that
when you weren't even looking.

In Sunday school, the rabbi told us
that God was invisible. It was a sin
even to draw a picture of Him
or to say His name out loud.
If you did, you'd die on the spot.
But here I was, staring at God, holding God,
and I was still on this planet breathing.
My best friend, Janet Crosio, had the same
statue on a shelf in her living room:
I'd thought it was one of her mother's knickknacks;
I never dreamed that it was God.

Mary told me God's name—Jesus Christ—
and that his mother's name was Mary, too.
But Mary—my Mary—was sixteen, Italian,
a high school dropout, a heavy smoker
who lived in a boardinghouse, alone.
Why my mother had hired her, I don't know.
I quickly slipped God back to her.
And while I waited to be taken home,
still amazed that I'd seen God,
I stared out of the second-story window
at an ugly concrete yard below.

On the windowsill Mary's glass ashtray
overflowed with ashes and cigarette butts.
I wasn't thinking, something came over me—
I blew into the ashtray, and ashes flew
into my eyes, a whirlwind of ashes
stinging and burning, gritting up under my eyelids.
Rubbing only made it worse.
I had to cry the ashes out, every last one—
tears like burning rain.
I had to be blind for the hour or so
until I could see again without hurting.
Since then, I often confuse revelation and pain.

CRAZY JOEY

Crazy Joey was famous,
more famous than the mayor.
Though he was as old as my father,
and tall and clean shaven,
he wore his navy blue stocking cap
pulled way down over his ears,
dressed for winter even in June.

What was he doing
hanging around the school yard,
slowly pedaling his dented Schwinn
just as school was letting out?
He'd pick a kid. Boy or girl.
He'd wait until you turned the corner.
Then, he'd follow you home on his bike,
an empty red milk crate strapped
to its back fender.

There were rumors
that he lived with his mother in a basement.
Rumors that he was born wrong end first.
Rumors that his father beat him senseless.
Rumors that some eighth-grade boys
lured him into an alley, and made him
pull down his pants and pee,
and that Crazy Joey did it, cheerfully.

When, in the seventh grade, my turn came,
I pretended to ignore him,
clutching my homework, my empty lunchbox,
never once turning my head.
Crazy Joey trailed me
past the used-car lot and the deli,
through the neighborhood
neither of us lived in,
grid of locked garages, neat shoe-box lawns,
house after house after house
like televisions all tuned to the same station.

It wasn't my fault
I studied piano and ballet.
It wasn't my fault
both my parents were alive.
It wasn't my fault
I was normal, even though
I lived in an apartment over our store,
and not in a real house, either.

So I didn't take the shortcut,
or try to hide, or run crying to my father
rolling up the awning of our store,
but watched my every careful step
the day Crazy Joey chose me.

MRS. HITLER

When my mother got into a bad mood,
brooding for days,
clamping her jaws shut, refusing to talk,
brushing past me, angry,
on her way to the kitchen,
I'd call her "Mrs. Hitler" under my breath.

I knew it was wrong, very wrong.
But when my mother turned around,
I'd stick out my tongue
at Mrs. Hitler in her blue nylon nightgown
and pink foam hair rollers,
glaring at the dishes in the sink.
Sometimes, I'd give her the finger, hiding
my hand behind my back,
although I knew it was wrong, very wrong.

Hitler had killed Anne Frank
whose diary was required reading
in my junior high.
My father had fought Hitler during the War.
But the first time I heard Hitler's name
I was hovering outside the kitchen,
eavesdropping on my aunts
sitting around our dinner table,
whispering about "the Jewish camps."
When I burst into the room,
they switched from talking English
to Yiddish, to me pure gibberish,
my ear a funnel for their gravelly words.

Were they planning to send me back
to Camp Bell, the Jewish day camp
I'd gone to the summer before?
Homesick, I'd lost my appetite
and five pounds, refusing to eat.
If they sent me back,
I'd go on another hunger strike.

I'd seen the *Life* magazine
hidden in my parents' bedroom—
seen the photographs of Jews,
all skin and bones,
and a picture of Hitler
and his little black push-broom mustache.

And I'd seen an old newsreel on TV:
German soldiers dressed
in gray uniforms, blocks of them marching,
taking giant steps in unison
as if they were playing
Follow the Leader with their friends.

I made up my own game then.
While my mother cooked dinner,
I'd sit on the kitchen floor,
with a plate and a knife
and a big chunk of Muenster cheese,
and pretend I was a Jew starving to death
like the Jews I saw in *Life*.

The cheese supply allotted me—
like my father's Marine rations—
was to last exactly thirty days:
I divided my cheese into a grid
cut into thirty pieces,
I popped a tiny cube into my mouth
like taking my daily vitamin,
and gobbled it down, then whispered,
so my mother couldn't hear,
"I was very hungry, thank you."

A moment later, I'd gruffly reply,
"You're welcome," pretending
to be my jailer, a Nazi guard;
taking on both roles, both voices,
at once—one high, one low—
just like when I played with dolls.

Day Two dawned a minute later.
My breakfast, lunch, and dinner
melted in my mouth.
"Thank You." "You're welcome."
Day Three followed, and so on,
as I played my game, Concentration Camp.

And I fed myself
the way a mother feeds her baby.
And I ate and I ate and I ate
until all the food on my plate was gone.

THE UNCANNY

Saturday afternoons, they like
having me over—
having had no children together
of their own.

Late afternoon, the venetian blinds
stripe gold prison bars
on their white satin bedspread:

both of them dressed
in casual slacks and pastel golf shirts;
they played eighteen holes
earlier today.

Door ajar, I burst in,
about to ask them a question.
He sits on his side
of the bed, facing the blinds,
his back to me,
his head tilting up to hers
leaning down, as if to kiss him.

He turns and, for an instant,
I see it—see her tenderly
swabbing the empty socket
of his missing right eye, her Q-Tip
poised over the flat planes of his face
as if she's about to dot an *i*.

Losing so precious an organ
is my uncle's punishment—
a married man with two children—
for having had an affair with my aunt
before he married her.

She has to clean it every single day;
and every single day,
she changes the patch.

Al met Aunt Flossie
a few years after he'd married Tess,
who isn't a real aunt
although I call her that.

I didn't used to think it odd
that he lived in a house with Tess
and his kids, but some days
he visited with my aunt.

For twenty-six years
they acted like an old married couple
until, one day, Aunt Flossie and Uncle Al
made it legal.

When he wears his formal black eye patch,
Al looks like Moshe Dayan.
He couldn't get a glass eye
to replace it, one like Sammy Davis Jr.'s.
He had a little tear on his bottom lid
they couldn't sew up.

Thirteen years before I was born,
driving between Aunts Flossie and Tess,
he fell asleep at the wheel.
My mother says Al is lucky
all he lost that night
was an eye.

I catch a glimpse, just as
Flossie is about to cover it
with a folded square of gauze
cut in the oval shape of an eye.
Gently, she pulls adhesive tape from a roll,
cuts the sticky white strip
into two equal lengths,
makes a big sticky X
to lay across the gaping socket
and hold the gauze in place.

She is the one who sees me first.
Surprised. When he turns to face me,
flashing his one good eye,
my aunt quickly covers
his nakedness. But it's too

late, I've already seen—
where the other eye should be—
the wrinkled pocket of skin
I've always been so curious about.

DIARY

On Thursday night, January 1, 1959,
I locked my diary's gold-plated lock
with a tiny gold-plated key that I would wear
on a gold-plated chain around my neck
for the whole next year
so my mother couldn't read the lists
of dirty jokes (titles only),
my favorite songs, crushes on boys,
and where I'd practiced signing
my future married name—
  Mrs. Marty Dubowsky
  Mrs. Martin Dubowsky
  Mrs. Jane Dubowsky
  Mr. and Mrs. M. Dubowsky—
in my best handwriting on the flyleaf.

On the powder blue leatherette cover,
in thick black Magic Marker I'd printed
PRIVATE! KEEP OUT! THIS MEANS YOU!
and I meant her.
Because when Ava's mother read Ava's diary
without Ava's permission,
picked the lock with a bobbie pin,
read about Ava kissing Teddy Lane,
our school's one and only Puerto Rican,
at the Embassy Theater's Saturday matinee,
she slapped Ava across the face
and grounded her for a month.

Ava was "mature for her age," my mother said.
Ava wore the same size bra cup
my mother wore now.
"Raisins on Pancakes"—
that's what the boys in school called me
behind my back, even to my face.

Once a week,
I would lock myself in the bathroom
with an Old-Fashioned glass
I'd stolen from my father's bar.
Hitching up my undershirt,
I'd stick the cold tumbler
over my left breast, the bigger one,
to see if it had grown
since the last time I measured.
Maybe this time I'd get up the courage
to beg my mother to buy me a bra,
the padded kind
the other flat-chested girls wore.

Mornings, sampling her lipsticks,
I'd see that disgusting thing—
the brick-red rubber douche bag—
my mother sometimes draped
dripping on the showerhead.
Like a glazed Peking duck hanging
in a grocer's window in Chinatown,

the long looping tube of its wrung neck
ended in a beak—the plastic nozzle
drooping down between the hot and cold faucets.

Once, when I'd asked her
what she used it for, she answered,
without looking in my eyes,
"Personal hygiene," but I knew.

Late at night, pretending to be asleep,
I'd hear the bathroom lock click
and faintly running water, and I'd imagine her
sitting on the toilet
and sticking that nozzle—
I was too shy to ask her exactly where.
She was my mother, I was her daughter.
She had her secrets, I had mine.

THE BEST-DRESSED GIRL IN SCHOOL

"I could make you the best-dressed girl in school,"
my mother used to say. "But I won't.
Better that you're famous for something else,
like getting good grades
or having the best manners in your class."

My mother was famous.
She owned the best dress shop in town.
At thirteen, I could almost fit
into the size 3 petites
that hung in our store downstairs,
directly under my bedsprings.
So what, if a dress hung loose on me.
Why was my mother so stingy?

The first week of school,
she drove to Little Marcie's Discount Clothes.
I didn't want any of my friends
catching my mother shopping there.
She beamed as she dumped the bag out
on my bed, my new fall wardrobe
piled high as a pasha's pillows:

pajamas and panties and argyle socks,
white cotton blouse with Peter Pan collar,
red tattersall jumper, dungarees,
and a blue plaid woolen skirt.

Inside every collar and waistband,
the fraying outline where the label
had been razored out.
"Don't turn up your nose," my mother said.
"What gives *you* the right to be a snob?"

The following Sunday, unfolding
the blue plaid skirt from its bag,
she made me stand on a kitchen chair
while she chalked the endless circle of pleats.
Pins scratching my knees, she put up my hem.
Monday morning, I
and five other girls in Mrs. Cooper's class
sat wearing Little Marcie's blue plaid skirt,
just like girls in parochial school uniforms.

But not Stacie,
the best-dressed girl in my school,
who bought her clothes at Lord & Taylor.
I wanted what Stacie had—
her Pendleton skirts and Lanz nightgowns,
her London Fog raincoat and Bass Weejuns—
and Stacie's mother, instead of mine.

Stacie's mother spoiled her, my mother said,
because Stacie was "plain,"
and her grades "just average."
"She doesn't have anything else going for her,"
my mother said, "other than clothes."

Hypocrite! My mother's whole life
was about clothes!
Buying, selling, wearing, breathing, eating,
sleeping, talking clothes!
Like a musician with perfect pitch,
my mother had a natural talent for clothes.

She grew up during the Depression.
She'd had to work and work
to get to where she was today—
the owner of the best dress shop in town—
but she was sick of clothes.
Sundays, summers, Christmas eves,
she could never take a vacation
away from clothes.

Her customers waited for her
in their dressing rooms,
in the separate stalls
behind dark green corduroy curtains,
barefoot, in their bras and slips,
waited for her
to run to the racks and bring them back
the perfect garment to try on.

And I waited, too,
apprenticed to my mother's exquisite taste.
Sweeping the floor
or stacking flat hosiery boxes
behind the counter, I'd climb on a stool

so I could better see
my mother tease a woman's arm
into a silk sleeve of a blouse,
or help her step into a skirt,
or pull a gabardine sheath over her hips,
or drape her in challis—

I watched my mother
button them up and zip them down.
I watched her dress the entire town.
Everyone in town, but me.

On Tuesdays, when she changed the windows,
the regulars dropped by to see
what she put on the mannequins.
Browsing in the store,
they'd pinch me on the cheek and say,
"You'll be a lucky girl, when you grow up."
I wasn't so sure that it was luck.

She was the queen;
I, the heir.
It would have been a snap for her
to make me the best-dressed girl in school.
But for me she wanted better.

"Give me, give me," I'd say in my head.
And my mother would answer
as though she'd heard me,
"If I give you all these dresses now,
what will you want when you're fifteen?"

THE PRINCESS OF THE RINK

Stacie and I skated on Hudson County Lake
on Mondays when her father's rink was closed.
She, in her short Sonja Henie skirt, and I,
in my dungarees and long johns.
She skated wobbly circles around me,
crooked figure eights, then she'd fall
in the middle of her death spiral.
Limping to the skating shed,
she unlaced her fancy figure skates,
her cheeks pink from showing off.

When I'd walk her home, Stacie's mother—
in black negligee and feathered mules—
would be waiting at the door
with Stacie's skim milk and diet cookie.
Mrs. D. wore her mink stole to shop at the A & P.
On the High Holidays, her cleavage
parted the congregation's dark-suited sea.
"What a waste," my mother said,
"so much money and so little taste."
And so little to do all day
what with Stacie's father away at business,
managing a franchise of Sonja Henie's,
whose hand Stacie had shaken personally,
and whose autographed 8-by-10 glossy
she'd thumbtacked to her bedroom wall.

Stacie had skating practice twice a week
and a closetful of sequined costumes
she'd squeeze into, for competitions.
I wanted skating lessons,
but added to piano and ballet,
my mother said enough was enough.
I had to help out in our store:
fold boxes, straighten dresses,
be on my best behavior
with our salesgirls, Eleanor and Josie—
best friends, just like Stacie and me.

I'd go, sometimes, to Stacie's lessons
and skate by myself in a corner of the rink.
Once, when she attempted the double lutz,
the coach stamped his foot and called Stacie
a *klutz*, the boss's daughter!
The bell rang. All skaters cleared the ice.
The Zamboni machine roared broad sweeps
across the ice as Stacie's eyes
glazed over with tears.
But Stacie didn't argue. Or complain. Or tattle.
An amiable, sweet-tempered girl,
she knew she had to set a good example.
She was the Princess of the Ice Palace, just as I
was the Princess of Corduroy Village.

One Monday, the lake too thin to skate on,
Stacie's mother took us shopping.
At the wheel of her silver Cadillac Coupe de Ville,
with her sunglasses and cigarette holder,
she looked like Gina Lollobrigida.
I was thrilled to be part of the entourage
as its star and embarrassed starlet
pulled into the lot at Lord & Taylor.

I watched the shoe salesman kneel
to measure Stacie's pale white feet,
watched him carry out box after box
from the storeroom, watch him fish out
the tissue paper stuffed into the toes,
watched him slip Stacie two shriveled nylon peds
and ease the shoes on, watched blushing Stacie march
before the mirror while Stacie's mother charged
four pairs of shoes to her account.

A week later, Stacie broke her ankle, skating.
I paid her a call, bearing a bag
of sugar-free sourballs.
The shoeboxes were piled like cinderblocks
at the foot of her mattress,
the sandwich on her lunch tray
reduced to crumbs.

Tacked above the headboard, Sonja Henie
posed in a sit-spin on glossy ice,
in a short skirt and flesh-colored tights,
her right leg extending toward the camera,
the white boot of her skate
like the thick plaster cast
wrapped around Stacie's foot and ankle
propped up on pillows
higher than her heart.

Stacie grinned; she'd have to stay off her feet
until she learned to use her crutches.
She'd have to miss two weeks of school,
six months of practice, and sit out
the regional championship.
Pointing at the stiff right leg of her jeans
slit cuff to knee along the seam,
she handed me a fountain pen.

Between patches of black and blue ink
where other friends had signed her cast,
I wrote my autograph,
the pen nib skating on the white carapace
covering the tender, itchy skin
Stacie scratched at with a chopstick,
trying to reach the deeper hurt
beneath that compliant flesh.

MY MOTHER'S SPACE SHOES

My mother's feet were always killing her.
All day she stood in the store
selling dresses, hobbling to the dress racks
like a Chinese woman with bound feet.

My mother's mother died of the 1918 flu.
My mother was a baby.
Raised by her grandmother, aunts,
and older sisters, my mother inherited
their brown hair, their nice figures,
their hand-me-down dresses
and their old cramped shoes.

And so her toes grew crooked and her arches fell.

I was twelve when she bought her first pair
of orthopedic space shoes. Custom made,
they cost one hundred dollars, plus tax.
She had to go to the factory in Manhattan
and stand still for fifteen minutes,
ankle-deep in a pan of wet plaster of Paris.
Six weeks later, the shoes arrived—
flats molded in the exact shape of her feet,
the hard, black leather already broken in,
bulging with hammer toes and bunions,
and grained like a dinosaur's skin.

She clomped to the cash register,
she clomped to hand a customer a dress.
At noon, she clomped to the deli
and ordered a corned beef sandwich,

her rubber soles leaving a trail
of black scuffmarks on their waxed linoleum.
I was embarrassed for her. It was worse
than wearing bedroom slippers in public.

Six o'clock, she clomped upstairs
and cooked us dinner, and after dinner—
my father dozing on the sofa,
my sister and I sprawling on the floor
in front of the TV—
my mother plopped down in her easy chair
with her cigarettes and newspaper,
and soaked her feet
in a dishpan of soapy water.

Why couldn't she keep her pain to herself?
I cringed, trying to ignore the sounds she made
torturing herself with a pedicure—
using the fancy cuticle cutters, scissors,
clippers, and pumice stone bought
from the Hammacher Schlemmer catalogue.
An hour later, her feet were done,
wrinkly pink, like a newborn's.
She powdered her toes with Dr. Scholl's;
only then, could I breathe normally again.

My mother was wearing her space shoes
the day I bought my first high heels
at Schwartz & Son's, where I'd gone
since I was a toddler, the only store in town
with an X-ray machine
that showed if your shoes fit properly
and your feet had room enough to grow.

Young Mr. Schwartz jammed my big toe
against the metal sliding ruler.
Five double A, I'd grown
a whole half-size since last spring.
He brought out the pair of ugly
"sensible shoes" my mother chose—
squat heels and square toes,
and the ones I wanted—
pointy-toed, black patent leather.

Two inches taller in those shiny pumps,
I teetered across the carpet, triumphant.
But with every step, the pointy toes pinched.
Old Mr. Schwartz conducted me
to the X-ray console that only he
knew how to operate. I stepped up
on the pedestal, slid my feet
into the box, and peered down.

And saw my right foot and my left foot
side by side, twin mummies,
skeletons visible through their wrappings,
bones glowing ghostly green and webbed
with grayish flesh, the cloudy ectoplasm
of squeezed ligaments and tendons.

Like my mother,
I was wearing myself inside out.
Like her standing in that pan of plaster,
I was stuck with myself forever,
wincing, rocking backward on my heels.

OVER SEXTEEN

Aunt Flossie, I remember exactly where
Over Sexteen stood in your den, black spine
squeezed between your battered *Webster's*
and sauce-spattered *Joy of Cooking,* and how,
like a library book, it reappeared
in the same location week after week
as if catalogued by magic, and how,
the minute I opened the door to your
apartment, your love nest, where Uncle Al
kept dropping in before you finally
married him, I'd head straight for
the third shelf above the color TV,
flop down on the sofa, plump up the pillows,
and read while eating my corned beef on rye,
read while sitting on the toilet to pee,
read while wiping myself, not even
the Atomic Bomb dropped on North Bergen
could have shaken me from my concentration
on the jokes about foreplay and afterglow,
jokes about the farmer's daughter, jokes
about Tom, Dick, and Harry, cherry jokes,
sexist jokes, "fairy" jokes, enema jokes
hilarious to a girl of twelve.
I memorized the text's sight gags and puns
as though you were going to test me on them,
I studied those punch lines and dirty
drawings, captions, and off-color limericks
as if researching a term paper for school,
thumbing through cartoons of couples talking—
husbands and wives, lechers and virgins,

doctors and nurses, bosses and secretaries,
big-bosomed bimbos, bald-headed nebbishes—
thought balloons floating over their heads
like blown-up condoms filled with words.
Yet never a curse or four-letter word,
bare tit, or curlicue of pubic hair.
A couple, invisible, under the sheets,
in a dark bedroom. One says to the other:
"If I didn't love you, would I be doing this?"
A couple groping in the pitch black dark:
"Oh pardon me. I thought it was the bedpost."
A baby chick, hatching from an egg, a dazed
expression on its face: *"I just got laid!"*
A male plug chasing a female socket
up a hill, their "private parts" exposed:
*"When the lights go on again, all over
the world."* Did people really behave like them?
You and Uncle Al, for example, tuning
your attention to the pro-golf match
on TV, ignoring me sprawled on your sofa—
raptly reading—my Clearasil-dotted nose
stuck in your juicy book. I couldn't
imagine you two bouncing on your king-size
Beautyrest, engaging in the polysyllabic
acts I'd had to look up in the dictionary,
my vocabulary improving by the week.
"Bookworm!" you'd teased me, until my body
went away to college and learned the facts
of life, firsthand. No how-to manual,
Joy of Sex, Story of O, Kama Sutra,

Kinsey Report, no Masters and Johnson, no
Eustace Chesser, M.D.'s *Love Without Fear:*
How to Achieve Sexual Fulfillment
in Marriage, (the dusty tome my parents
must have consulted on their wedding night,
following its instructions to the letter—
"insert A into B, manipulate C—"
as if constructing a model airplane.)
Parents, *schmarents!* They never knew
what I was doing, thanks to you.
Flossie, you were my aunt, not my mother,
mainly because you *weren't* my mother,
you let me lie on your couch all day—
week after week, year after year—
educating myself.

A NIGHT IN SHANGRI-LA

Hurrying home from the gym a few hours
before my junior prom, I tripped
on the cracked sidewalk outside school.
I knew right away it was a pretty bad fall.
An egg-size lump and big black-and-blue mark
popped out of my lower right shin,
trapping the black jelly of clotted blood.
Ice packs didn't bring the swelling down.
When my mother saw my leg she said *Forget the prom.*
But it was too late to cancel.
I had a dress. My date was on his way.
Head of the decorating committee,
I'd stained my fingers purple
making hundreds of crepe-paper flowers
after school for weeks before the prom.

Stretching the sheer casing of my nylon
over the plump sausage of my aching calf,
I hooked my stocking to my garter belt
and slipped into my silk organza gown,
the long skirt and petticoat hiding my ugly leg
from the date I hardly knew, a gentle
brainy boy, a head taller than I,
imported from a high school in the Bronx.
He was cute, I could show him off.
He'd rented a tux, borrowed his father's car,
made a reservation at the Copacabana
for our night out on the town after the prom.

Himalayan scrim masked cinder-block walls,
a neon moon hung from the shot clock.
Leaning on his arm, I hobbled past
the rented wooden bridge and bower,
blushing couples lining up behind us
to have a formal picture taken.
When the photographer said to smile, a flashbulb
caught my grimace, caught the hemorrhage
of purple petals on my wrist—
the orchid the boy paid five dollars for
and transported across state lines, on ice—
caught the hurt expression on his face,
the dazed one on mine, still a little foggy
from aspirin and from pain.

I had just finished telling him
a little white lie.
The real reason was too embarrassing.
I told him I had a fever
and felt too sick to dance.

Thinking back on it now, I'd probably
broken the bone—a hairline fracture.
Thirty years later, it's still a little tender.
I can feel the bump when I'm shaving my legs
or putting on a pair of panty hose.
A doctor would have kept me home.
Although I wouldn't dance, I could walk,
could limp to our table where we sat

stiffly all evening with chaperones
watching couples stumble across the dance floor
like the dazed survivors of an air crash
escaping out the side door, in feverish twos,
into the parking lot's dark cars.

He plucked me a paper flower
to keep as a souvenir.
A gentleman, he never complained,
and he never called me again.
Ace Rental picked up the bridge on Monday.
Back in its white cardboard box,
his corsage lasted a week in my refrigerator.
Under my skirt, my flowering bruise.

TWO

NEXT DAY (1969)

"Bitching about the price of cheese,
the hateful avocado and other small
luxuries, insisting on my pinch's
worth of melon, say, ten years
after the big move west, the MA,
kids, and husband off lecturing
at the university, the split
will be the same split, even here.
To risk the fierce delicious rite
of openness—rushing to the comfort
of a private man, alone, a quick
elaborate affair that celebrates
release, the word that stuns us
into motion: to risk this
would be to risk too much.

"Adapting so exquisitely to careful
lists of recipes and calories,
a woman closes up. And closing
in, I live a little distance
from myself, avoid the ease
with which the flesh takes on
weight and sentiment, the falling away
of time, my shrinking vocabulary.
The baby rides shotgun
in the jump seat, mauling heads
of lettuce. The elder daughter,
my smudged and spidery replica,
taunts the triggered door; tests
the impossibility of choice."

(1989)

Twenty years later in the same Grand Union,
wheeling my baby daughter down the aisle,
I see a girl meandering in Produce,
a college student from my old school.

On top of her shaved head, a spiky nest.
Breasts jiggling under unzipped leather vest.
Army boots. I pass, wincing at her pierced
eyebrow, her left cheek etched with a tattoo.

Glancing at my jeans, my Birkenstocks, my baby,
my graying hair shagged and hennaed red,
she turns back to her organic scallions.
I know what she is thinking. *I* thought so, too:

when she grows old, she'll *never* be like me.
At loopy Goddard, the facts fell
straight from Dewey: *Learn by doing.*
My senior year, smoking dope, reading Keats,

embroidering rainbows on my bell-bottoms,
ironing my long hair straight as Joan Baez's,
I was weighing poetry and marriage,
trying to imagine myself in twenty years.

Isn't it true that poetry drives you crazy?
Take Plath and Sexton, my old role models.
What do you call a woman poet's muse?
Put yourself into your mother's shoes.

I used to think about poetry in the library.
Now I worry about what to make for dinner.
Dare I buy mesclun at five dollars a pound,
chicken tenders, skinned and boned?

But I wrote poems, chose "the life of art,"
though "chose" isn't entirely the right word,
because life and art were equal pulls.
How much was fate, and how much will?

That Goddard girl and I cross paths again
before the freezer chest of Healthy Choice.
I'm old enough to be her mother. Maybe
she thinks I'm my daughter's grandmother!

She's thinking middle-aged ex-hippie,
ex-yuppie, ex-patriate from the city.
What does she know? She's probably
as dumb as I was, at her age.

Waiting on the shortest checkout line,
I scan a tabloid's headline:
WOMAN, 92, GIVES BIRTH TO TWINS.
A baby boomer, a late bloomer,

I had my "miracle baby" at forty-one,
ten years later than my poem predicted.
Should I feel guilty she's an only child?
I had one. Should I have had two?

Was *that* the cost of making art?
But how prescient of me, at twenty-two,
to divide myself in two—two daughters—
like the two choices I was split between:

an artist testing the mirrored door of art,
or her passive baby-self being wheeled
in the fold-down seat of a shopping cart.
The trapped housewife in the supermarket

I dreaded that I would one day be,
chose safe domesticity, and was sorry.
Life or art—she felt she couldn't have both,
paralyzed by the impossibility.

My mother was split between her home
and her business, between upstairs
and downstairs, apartment and store,
never completely happy in either,

guilty in both, caught between stories—
should she be downstairs working
or upstairs with us? What did it cost her,
a "working mother," before her time?

So I'm a writer. Is that better?
And I have a daughter. Is that better?
Was it a willful choice, or wasn't it?
How much was will, how much fate?

Meeting my husband late in life.
But if I'd met him twenty years earlier?
Writing poems, before and after.
But if I hadn't had the jobs I had?

I chose. And life chose. Like my mother,
I'm still split between the two.
My baby coos, sucking on a breadstick.
Nadezhda Mandelstam quotes Akhmatova—

"What makes you think you *ought* to be happy?"
Twenty years later in the same Grand Union,
living five miles from my former dorm,
I'm having a little déjà vu,

remembering myself imagining my future,
a prophesy that came partly true.
And now, like a multiple orgasm,
another epiphany begins to come:

my Present is quickly learning
what my Past already knew.
Zipping through Express: 10 Items or Fewer,
the girl turns and flashes me

a V sign for victory, or peace,
or maybe it's a secret signal?
She's me at twenty, minus the hair,
and wearing her pierces on the outside.

If I were her, by now I would have had
my nipple ring, and my lesbian affair.
She tucks her wallet into her boot,
smiles at me, and waves good-bye.

I pile my groceries on the moving belt.
Paper or plastic? I'll bag them myself,
boxes of Total, Life, a tub of Promise.
In the antechamber of the Grand Union,

two pairs of glass automatic doors
pop open and shut like heart valves.
Motion sensors. They'll open
for me, they'll open for anyone.

Pushing my cart, I catch my reflection,
reflections—there are more than one—
coming and going through these doors
that, a decade from now, will shut

behind me as I enter the millennium,
leaving behind the woman standing in line,
leaving behind the divided girl I was
when I wrote that poem in 1969.

THE TRAP

"Why didn't you just break its neck?"
That's what I asked him the morning after
its cries kept us awake all night.

When I moved into his Tribeca loft,
he was between marriages, and I—
I was hungry for something.

He was cordial on the phone to his ex-wife,
with whom he shared joint custody
of boys, nice boys, ages ten and twelve.

Both of them had a crush on me.
Three nights a week, they'd sleep
in the plywood alcove above our bed,

their tree house stocked with the duplicate
comforts and clutter of home—
comic books, games, Legos, toys—

while below, their guilty father and I
would slide the shoji screens shut
and make love without breathing.

His designer loft was divided into areas,
not rooms, so I had to imagine walls,
had to invent my privacy when his sons

spied on me through the bathroom's
smoky Plexiglas partition, staring
as I sat on the toilet, shaved my legs,

or bathed in the deep redwood tub.
One morning when I was toasting
an English muffin, a mouse shot out

of the toaster slot and scampered off,
tail singed where it had curled itself,
asleep against the dormant wires.

That's when I began to notice brown
caraway seeds sprinkled on the tops
of cereal boxes, soup cans, rattling

inside coffee mugs. Mouse shit. And confetti-
colored mouse shit, like jimmies,
after they'd gnawed on a box of crayons.

Getting rid of them was my obsession.
Pretty blue pellets that the exterminator
scattered behind the sink and under the stove

were crumbs leading out of the forest;
the poison they carried back to the nest
and fed to the litter was guaranteed

to make them thirsty, delirious to drink,
desperate to return to water
in the cellar, gutter, sewer, river.

I stuffed steel wool around the pipes,
baited mousetraps with graying hamburger.
By summer, something was dying

inside the walls, something we'd catch
a whiff of, fighting in loud whispers
under the quilt late at night,

mice scurrying up and down the turnpike
between the bed and stripped brick wall
sieving mortar grit onto the pillows.

Four floors over a notions factory,
the clanking cage of the freight elevator
stalled between floors, I memorized

the locks on the loft's only door:
the police lock's long steel rod
jammed into a hole drilled into the floor,

the Medeco steel bar, the dead bolts,
cylinders, latches, and sliding chains.
We'd wake to a loud snap, then silence

behind the radiator, he'd get up
grumbling, and dispose of his catch
as he always did, lifting the lid,

and flushing it down the toilet.
But that night he carried a dying mouse
to the bathroom—its neck still caught

between the trap's snapped jaws—
why do I think it gave him pleasure
as he filled the sink with water

and floated the mousetrap—
the animal, anchored to the balsa raft,
frantically paddling on an oval lake

until it finally drowned.
Those paralyzing cries kept us awake;
neither of us able to make the final break.

EVIL EYE

When my daughter was two,
watching *The Wizard of Oz* on television,
the moment the Wicked Witch appeared in a scene,
Emma would walk, as if hypnotized,
to the glowing screen and kiss
the witch's luminous green face
in the same placating way
my mother used to kiss the little silver hand,
the charm she wore on a chain around her neck.

The day Emma was born, my mother
bought a yard of narrow red satin ribbon.
She tied a bow, several bows,
and basted the loops together in the middle
until they formed a big red flower
she Scotch-taped to the head of Emma's crib
to protect her while she slept.
My mother made a duplicate,
in case I lost the first one,
to pin onto the carriage hood.
"You can never be *too* safe," she said.

My mother used to coo in Yiddish over the crib,
"*Kine-ahora, kine-ahora,*
my granddaughter's so beautiful."
And then suddenly as if remembering something,
something very bad, she'd go *"pui pui pui"*,
pretending to spit three times on the baby's head.

My mother wasn't some fat *bubbe* from the shtetl.
She owned a business, drove a car.
I'd never seen her act this way before.

Sitting at her kitchen table, she lit another Kent.
"You should have given Emma an ugly name
to ward off the evil eye.
Harvey Lebow, the brilliant young concert pianist?
The evil eye was jealous, so it killed him.
Mrs. Cohen, who won the lottery
and went on a spending spree?
A week later, she had a miscarriage.
Remember Bonnie, the doctor's daughter,
your friend who died of leukemia
when you were growing up?
Her mother wore a floor-length mink;
they had a pinball machine
in their basement rec room.
That's like an open invitation."
My mother stubbed out her cigarette.

My hand fanned the smoke away.
"Ma, You don't really believe
in that hocus-pocus, do you?"

"Maybe not," she said, "but it doesn't hurt."

FAIRBANKS MUSEUM AND PLANETARIUM

We climb the stone staircase
of the red-stone Victorian building,
my father, my aunt, my husband carrying our baby,
escaping from the mid-July heat.
My mother is missing, dead one year.

Downstairs the museum, upstairs the planetarium;
we've waited over an hour
for the next star show to start,
rejected the brochures and guided tour,
killing time, instead, with the souvenir shop's
boxed binoculars and plastic bugs,
rocks and minerals, and packages
of stick-on, glow-in-the-dark stars.

We loiter past the Information Desk
where they've set up a card table with an exhibit
of local flora, each wildflower—
stuck in its own glass jar
propping up a smudged typewritten label:
QUEEN ANNE'S LACE, COW VETCH, wilting BLACK-EYED SUSANS—
sprinkling pollen on the tabletop
like pinches of curry power.

The high barrel-vault ceiling made of oak,
the oak woodwork and oak balconies
shiny as the beautiful cherry and glass cabinets
the janitor just finished polishing,
but all the exhibits inside the cases
are falling apart, from the loons' moth-eaten
chests molting like torn pillows,
to the dusty hummingbirds' ruby bibs.

We interrupt a custodian vacuuming
a stuffed polar bear with a Dust Buster.
The bear's down on the floor with us, on all fours,
pinning a seal under his mauling paw.
Shuttling the baby between us,
we shuffle past a grizzly
rearing up on his pedestal;
his shin fur scuffed and shiny
where visitors' fingers have touched.
He's in a permanent rage, his bared teeth
stained yellow-brown, as if from nicotine.

The Information Lady hands us over
to the Tour Guide.
And though it is only ourselves, and a grumpy
French-Canadian family with three wired kids
detoured from the Cabot Creamery,
she ushers us up the wooden staircase where we meet
the people from the twelve o'clock show
staggering down.

French doors open and close on the planetarium
barely bigger than a living room,
rows of wooden benches
orbiting the central console
where our bearded, pony-tailed Star Guide stands
and welcomes each one of us
with a damp handshake and a "Hi."

My family sits together in one row,
obedient children on a class trip.
We're present, all eyes and ears.
The sun sets, the darkness intensifies.
Our eyes adjust, our heads tilt back.
Suddenly the starless night sky, pitch black,
dark as the inside of a closet,
makes me feel like crying.
Not a splinter of light squeezes out
from under the French doors' crack.
My father and aunt immediately doze off.
They're tired, tired of missing
his wife, her sister. Now there's nothing
but a big black hole to hold us all together,
the gravitational pull of grief.

"Tim" tells us his name.
With no higher-up to direct him,
he's got his chance to play God.
He pivots at his podium, clears his throat,
and casts his flashlight baton
across his orchestra of incipient stars,
no music yet, just warming up;
only his voice and a thin beam of light
about to point out areas of interest.
My husband hands me our daughter
and I unbutton my blouse to nurse her.

Tim tells us how he used to chart the heavens
from his bedroom window in Ohio when he was a boy,
then he rehashes the *Star War Trilogy*—
that's what first hooked him on astronomy.

He tells us about his courtship of Annie,
the home birth of his baby . . .
Every once in a while he remembers
to mention a star.

My father snores softly. Nights and days
are swirling all around us, moons rise and set,
seasons turn, constellations twinkle
on the cracked ceiling above our heads.
Over the planetarium's slate roof
floats our familiar sky,
two Dippers, Big and Little,
and Jupiter, Mars, and the same old moon,
big and yellow as a wheel of cheddar,
preparing to rise from behind our hill.

An hour later,
like the paired fish in Pisces
swimming in the sky, the baby and I
are still at sea, too exhausted
to crawl along the bleachers and escape outside.
The sun pops up, pure Keystone Kops.
My aunt startles awake, gropes for her purse.
My father snores louder.
Fading, the Milky Way shakes over his bald spot—
covered, one year ago, by a yarmulke
as he stood in the cemetery under the trees—
under the big dome of heaven
where my mother now lives.

HOT TUB

After twenty laps in the pool,
I hurry shivering to the hot tub,
and descend its ladder backward,
easing myself into the water reluctantly,
self-consciously, the way I used to enter
dances in high school, the hot whirling
gymnasium full of bodies smelling of hair spray
and mouthwash, not chlorine.
The bubbler's set for ten minutes.
Water rages forth from five furious jets.

I join two women already simmering
in a pot of soup eight degrees hotter
than the human body's Normal.
We sit and face each other, riders on a bus,
keeping our expressions blank
on purpose. Every so often we flash each other
little embarrassed smiles.
We know we look ridiculous, with these
frothy bubble beards on our chins.

At the hot tub's rim, a man appears—
dark haired, hairy chested,
wearing shiny black nylon bikini briefs.
He dips his toe in, a hairy leg, lowers
his body into the churning water
up to his neck, anchoring himself on the ledge
opposite mine. Smiling, he greets us ladies in turn,
acting like he's the hot tub's maître d'.

He's not my type at all.
He looks like he likes to hang out in bars.
Shouldn't he be at work?
About forty, and paunchy, his left arm's tattooed with . . .
but I can't read it without my glasses.
Although, I did glimpse a swatch
of his back, tanned and peeling
from a vacation in the Islands—
Club Med, I'll bet.

In the parking lot, it's ten below.
Two feet of fallen snow
ossify under my station wagon's
salt-spattered chassis.

Is he sexy? His dark curly head, detached
from its stalk of neck,
bobs atop the shiny platter of water,
and I can picture the rest of him
in the roiling cauldron underneath.
Where's his wedding ring? My cheeks flush,
but not from the heat.
All of a sudden I remember
that I'm a married woman, a mother,
and a nice Jewish girl, believe me.

Should he glance at me, I'll pretend
I'm studying the spa's aqua wall tiles.
It's nothing personal—
that's how I want to keep it,
although we're sharing the same water,
same body fluids, probably.

Back in the fifties, you could catch polio
in swimming pools.
And in 1960s New Jersey,
when I was a teenager, fourteen,
cooling off in the deep end of the pool
under the watchful eye
of my boyfriend, Dickie Borden,
the lifeguard at Westmount Country Club—
I had to be careful about him, too.
Dickie Borden. Too good to be true.
A blond, blue-eyed Jew, with teeth
straight out of Pepsodent,
a Speedo skimpy as Tarzan's,
and smooth Coppertoned chest.

Handy at Dickie's feet, ropes, nets,
life preservers, long aluminum poles—
the paraphernalia of rescue.
If I got into trouble,
Dickie could dive in and save me,
resuscitate me mouth-to-mouth,
flat on my back on the wet concrete,
in front of all the adults, in public;

and not in his locked cabana
with its damp wall of souring towels
against which Dickie's kisses pushed me
during his rushed fifteen-minute breaks,
where, once, I think I accidently touched—
through the cold cloth of his bathing trunks,
through the soft nylon liner
under the cotton shell—
his penis or something, knobby and warm.

I'm sweating. My blood's boiling.
Too much heat is bad for the heart.
The timer's run out.
Bubbler silent, the water suddenly calms,
turns greenish, brackish, and I can see
on the murky bottom four pairs of feet,
bleached and ugly as corpses',
flat by the drain near a rusting bobbie pin.
I fish out the thermometer dangling underwater.
With a fever this high,
by now, we'd all be dead.

SMALL TALK

On the drive back from dropping off
our daughter at sleep-away camp,
again a woman and a man,
we make small talk—
lake, cabins, canoes, cafeteria.

Take that blue Chevy in front of us—
that red Toyota tailgating behind—
a three-car cortege mournfully
inching along the logging road,
three sets of parents driving home
an empty backseat, slack seat belt,
empty trunk. Do you think they'll
jump into bed the minute they get there?
Tell me, when have we had a week alone together
since our daughter was born?

Home, I pay a visit to her room
formal as a doll museum.
Will the tent she's sleeping in
spring a leak, will she run out of
clean underwear, will they remember
to give her her allergy pills,
comb her hair? She's barely nine,
she's never been away from home
for more than a pajama party.

Remember that Thai café in Hawaii,
a month after she was born, the first time
we left her alone with a baby-sitter,
we'd try to behave like a couple
on a date, the very couple we were

four weeks before? But now
I ordered my food mild on purpose
so the spices wouldn't pass
into my milk and give her gas.

We nibbled Pad Thai, sipped ginger ale—
twirling the paper umbrellas in our drinks,
fiddling with our chopsticks,
checking the clock—
Was she hungry? Was she crying?
We lasted half an hour, then gave in.
"Emma!" we cried, repeating the name
together, same name I printed
with laundry pen this morning
on all the collars and waistbands
I stuffed into her duffel for camp.

The night she was born premature
in the hospital near Waikiki,
the night they cut me open, removed her,
and stitched me up again,
after the surgery and all the drugs,
I had a nightmare:
I was floating over a cemetery
by the sea in Hawaii,
over gravestones of black lava.

Now, again, she is separate from me.
As in the dream, my body,
suddenly lighter and free from gravity,
bounced from gravestone to gravestone,
the way at a party a balloon
is flicked from person to person
around the circle to keep it in the air.

SAWDUST

In front of our farmhouse
stand Charlotte, Valorus, Irene, and Helen,
hundred-year-old-plus sugar maples,
Will Peck planted one at a time
after each new child was born.

Today, we cut down Charlotte, I think.
She held up our hammock,
brushed our roof shingles,
shaded our front lawn.

Late October, rusting heaps of leaves
lie under a sky rubbed raw with storm.

Charlotte *looked* ill,
her trunk filigreed with lichen.
The pneumatic drill-bill
of a pileated woodpecker tore up her bark.
After last year's drought
and after years of acid rain,
we pumped a hundred gallons of fertilizer
in the ground around her roots,
water down a drain.

In the next big storm, if a dead branch fell
and crushed a passing car and killed someone,
we would be responsible.

Early this morning,
the Tree-works truck arrived
carrying two hard-hatted men and a crane.

After filling their chainsaws with gasoline,
the younger one climbed into the elevator bucket
lifting him high into the branches
where he lashed himself
like Odysseus to the mast,
while the other one, shouting from the ground,
operated the crane.

Then, like porcupines in heat,
they commenced their high-pitched
chainsaw mating call.

I had to stop my work.
High in the second-story bedroom,
my breath fogged the window
as I watched sawdust
fall on the grass like snow.

Soon Charlotte stood, a naked torso.
A deep V cut into her trunk, down low.

Then Charlotte fell.

After they cut the trunk into logs
and raked the lawn
and stacked the kindling
and fed the twigs and branches to the woodchipper
grinding so loud it hurt my teeth,

it was quiet, quieter than before.

Old Charlotte, old grandmother,
by late afternoon your stump eye
stared straight up into the clouds.

But for the first time we had
a clear view of the road,
the rising moon.

For the next two days,
our elderly neighbor, Morris,
stood in our front yard splitting firewood,
enough to help him through the winter—

his pounding ax,
a heartbeat's steady blows,
shaking and shaking our house.

"PUBLIC SERVICE IS RICH ENOUGH"

—that's what my mother used to say,
switching off the bathroom lights behind me.
"Public Service is rich enough," she'd nag,
when I'd leave the downstairs light on, in the hall.

Afternoons, I'd sit at the dining room table
and do my homework in the growing dark.
When I couldn't see another word,
I'd turn the chandelier dimmer on low,
then dial the lights bright as noon,
dimming them down to dusk, midnight,
and brightening the night to dawn again,
like God speeding through the first six days,
in a hurry to get some rest.

After my mother's funeral, my father and I
lit a tall, seven-day Yahrzeit candle
and put it on the stove, on a plate,
so it wouldn't catch their apartment on fire,
its flame nervous in the breeze I made
walking by, disturbing the progress
of my mother's soul on its way to heaven.

After my father died,
packing cartons, locking up the place for good,
I was surprised how dark it was, it always was.

"Public Service is rich enough,"
I mutter, trailing after my husband and my daughter,
griping at them as I douse the lights.

Sometimes, when we're out for the day
and come back after dark
and I've forgotten to turn the porch light on,
from the bottom of the hill our farmhouse
looks like a sooty shell,
and for a moment I think that it's burned down.

But if I've left a few lights on,
the house looks like it's on fire,
flames blazing from every window.
When we pull into the driveway,
and I peer through the screens at the empty rooms—
the open magazines on the coffee table,
unwashed plates in the sink, my breakfast
coffee cup rimmed with kiss marks—
I wonder whether we're really ghosts
occupying these brief parentheses.

My husband and daughter shuffle behind me
among the mudroom's scatter
of dirty boots and shoes.
I fumble for the key, open the door,
and burst in upon the kitchen's glare.
And as my family rushes past me,
tearing through the kitchen, the living room,
slamming up the stairs—
it's strange, how, for a moment—
those rooms, empty of them, seem suddenly darker.

REPRISE

Rummaging through the old cassettes my father
taped off the classical radio station,
my daughter finds, among Mozart and Bach,
catalogued and labeled in his elegant hand,
Jane's and Howard's Wedding: 1984.
I didn't know my father'd taped that, too!
Disappearing with the boombox, she shuts
the master bedroom's door. An hour later,
I walk in on her gate-crashing our wedding,
sprawling on our marriage bed, ear to the speaker.
When she was younger she used to insist
that *she* was present at our wedding, too,
and we've told her it's impossible,
she wasn't born yet, but that she was there
in spirit. She's not convinced, hasn't she
always been with us, even when she wasn't?

She laughs at the Wedding March while Howard
and I shakily walk down the aisle
under the rented yellow-and-white tent
filling Mike and Gail's Walnut Ave. backyard.
Eavesdropping on the prayers we repeat
after the rabbi, phrase by Hebrew phrase,
she claps when the rabbi pronounces us
husband and wife and we kiss to applause,
her future father stomps on the goblet
wrapped in the caterer's cloth napkin
and glass shatters safely underfoot.

She rewinds the tape back to the beginning,
to what she calls the "really funny part,"
back to before our murmuring guests
sit down in the rented chairs on that
sweltering June Sunday, 96 degrees,
freesia wilting, family close to fainting,
whipped cream on the cake about to turn,
back to before we stand under the canopy,
back to before the ceremony, back to when
my father presses the RECORD button, clears
his throat and says into the microphone:
"Testing. Testing."—a voice I last heard
five years ago, a few days before he died.

Shocked, I hear my dead mother say,
"George, are you sure the tape recorder's
working?" And my father answers, "I'm sure."
My mother says, "George, are you *sure*
the batteries aren't dead?" And my father
answers patiently at first, then wearily,
"Essie, I'm sure." She asks him again,
and he answers again, and here they are
arguing in my bedroom, in the house
my mother never set foot in.
My daughter's eyes shine with laughter;
mine with tears. Although I'd give anything
to have them back even for a moment, I clamp
my hands over my ears (just as I used to
when I was growing up) and shut them out again.

SHIT SOUP*

Other mothers have their "Everything Stew,"
"Icebox Ragout," "Kitchen-Sink Casserole."
Mine had "Shit Soup," a recipe she told me
standing in her kitchen in New Jersey.
"Find a big pot, the biggest pot you have.
Shit a quartered chicken into the pot.
If you have an old carcass lying around,
shit it in. Add three quarts of cold water
and salt, and bring to a boil. Skim off
the foam as it collects on the surface.
Halve one large or two medium onions.
Shit them in. Shit in some dill and parsley.
Dried is okay but fresh tastes better.
Cut into bite-size pieces some carrots,
a couple celery stalks. Shit them in.
Those lousy-looking zucchini squash,
withered wedges of cabbage, puckered peas.
In other words, anything in the fridge.
If you have fresh or frozen string beans,
shit them in. Shit in a few potatoes.
Peel the skin, dig out the eyes, cut off
the bad parts—and shit them in anyway—
they're filled with vitamins and minerals.
Friday's leftovers, oh, what the hell.
Shit them in, shit in twelve black peppercorns.
Want to know my secret ingredient?
One ripe tomato makes the broth taste sweet.
What's under that aluminum foil?
Shit it in. A little mold won't kill you.
My recipe? I don't measure. I just shit

a little of this in, a little of that.
Your Mama's Shit Soup. Enough for a week.
With a pot of this you'll never go hungry."
Shit in "There wasn't time for me to go
to the Shop-Rite and buy steaks to broil
for your father's and your dinner."
Shit in "I'd like to sell the store someday
and move to Florida." Shit in the Recession,
the Second World War, the Great Depression.
Shit in "There's no rest for the weary."
Shit in her bunions, her itchy skin.
Shit in "Rich or poor, it's nice to have money."
Shit in "Marriage isn't made in heaven."
Shit in the Republicans. Shit in her tumor.
Shit in where it spread to her liver
"like grains of rice," the doctor said.
Shit in her daughters at the cemetery
crying over the hole when they lowered
her in. Shit in one last handful of dirt.
Cover the pot and reduce heat to low.
Simmer on the lowest possible flame
for two hours, or until vegetables
are fork tender, meat falls off the bone.

In Yiddish, "shit-arein" means "to pour in."

MY MOTHER'S MIRROR

After her funeral, I swiped it,
swaddled it in tissue, and spirited it home.
I'd have preferred a plain unfussy one,
not this pewter cupid caryatid
bracing up a shining circle
flipping, two-faced, like a coin—
a regular mirror on one side,
a magnifying mirror on the other.

It was my mother's best friend,
worst enemy. As a girl, I watched her
stare into it for hours, examining
her wrinkles, tweezing her eyebrows.
Sometimes I'd walk in on her
inspecting her face pore by pore,
brow to chin. Once a week,

she'd smear her skin with a clay
beauty mask that hardened
white and smooth as porcelain,
broken only by the glittering peepholes
of her dark brown eyes.
She appraised her face
as if she were considering
a damaged antique vase, and weighing
the severity of its cracks.

Her jaw sagged, her chin doubled,
little bags puffed out
under her eyes.
Her right eye, then her left,
clouded over with cataracts.
The mirror never changed.

The day after her funeral, my sister
and I sat at our mother's dining table
and divided up her things.
I got the diamond engagement ring,
the longer string of pearls.
I was the older daughter, the first born.
I felt I had the right.

Now, at fifty,
I stare into her mirror
glazed with our common face,
the face I'll pass down to my daughter
who I sometimes see watching from behind me
with the same puzzled look I had
when I watched my mother,
out of the corner of her eye,
watching me.

But when I swivel the mirror
to its other side,
the face tilting back at me slides away
and returns twice its size,
with swollen nose, bulging eyes, unstable
flesh stretching like the taffy body
in the fun-house mirror
at Palisades Amusement Park
where I used to go and gaze
at the girl I was.

I look away. What did I think?
That I'd stay fourteen forever?
As my mother used to say,
"By the time you're fifty,
you get the face you deserve."

HAPPINESS

My friend Joyce opens her antique silk-covered box
and we shuffle twelve dozen ebony tiles
facedown on my kitchen table.
Joyce calls this the "Twittering of the Sparrows."
She's teaching my daughter, Emma, and me
how to play mah-jongg, the game
all the Jewish mothers played, except mine.

It's way past Emma's bedtime,
the harvest moon having risen hours ago
round and full as the one dot
on its tile of worn ebony.
After we've stacked the tiles
and built a square Great Wall of China,
Joyce hands Emma a tiny box carved from bone,
which holds two tiny ivory dice,
small as her baby teeth I tucked away
in an envelope in my keepsake drawer.

This is weird. My generation of women
wouldn't be caught dead playing mah-jongg,
the game all the Jewish mothers played,
summers at Applebaum's Bungalow Colony,
red fingernails clicking against the tiles.

Joyce's friend, Susan, taught her mah-jongg;
and like a big sister, Joyce wanted to teach me.
Her favorite bakelite bracelets
clunking noisily around her wrist,
she consults her tattered mimeographed sheets,
reading the rules out loud as we go along.

Beginners, we are not yet ready
to gamble with real money.
We lay our tiles faceup on the table,
exposing our hands, so everyone can see.

At Applebaum's my mother would watch
the other mothers playing mah-jongg—
but she wouldn't sit down and join them.
Even when she took the summer off,
my mother was not about playing.

I roll the highest score on the dice,
so I am the East Wind, the dealer.
But I'm sitting at the foot of the table,
where the south, on a map, would be.
It's not the normal geography.
The South Wind sits to the left of me
clunking her bracelets,
and Emma's the North Wind, on my right.
Joyce tells us a little trick to remember
the clockwise order of play—
"Eat Soy With Noodles,"
(East, South, West, North)—
and to remind us who'll be the East Wind next.

Oh how I love the sound of the tiles
clicking together, the sound our nails make
clicking against the tiles,
the sound the ebony tiles make
scraping the oak table, the sound the dice make
bouncing softly on the wood,

the sound my mouth makes calling out
"eight crack" and "five bamboo" as I discard them,
the sounds the ivory counting sticks make
when we add up our scores,
and the names of the hands we have scored,
syllables of pure pleasure:

combination of Pungs, Chows, Kongs,
and pillows, pairs of East Winds or Red Dragons,
making a Dragon's Tail, Windfall, LillyPilly,
Seven Brothers, Three Sisters, Heavenly Twins,
making a Green Jade, Royal Ruby, White Opal,
Red Lantern, and Gates of Heaven...

Why did my mother deny herself?
Once when I asked her, she confessed
that she never really enjoyed business.
I think that my mother
didn't much like mothering, either.
It scared her, too, the closeness of every day.
It was easier to fold my clothes
than to touch me. Even as she was dying,
she shut me out, preferring to be alone.
Now, she's like the West Wind in the empty chair
opposite me, the absent one we skip over
because we are playing with only three.

Emma shouts "Mah-jongg!"—she's won her first game.
Joyce is so thrilled, she forgets
we're not playing for money.

Rummaging in her purse, she pulls out
a dollar bill and crushes it into Emma's hand.
Emma flushes with pleasure.

We reshuffle the tiles. Twitter the sparrows—
all peacocks, dragons, flowers, seasons
hide under their black blankets of night.
Reflecting us, the dark window blurs our hands
then brightens into all the other hands I saw
around card tables set up under shade trees
during those long hot afternoons
in Rockland Lake, New York.
Babies napping, husbands away at work—
all the other mothers playing—
happy, sipping their iced drinks,
happy, smoking their cigarettes.

A NOTE ABOUT
THE AUTHOR

Jane Shore grew up in North Bergen, New Jersey. Her first book of poems, *Eye Level*, won the 1977 Juniper Prize; her second book, *The Minute Hand*, won the 1986 Lamont Poetry Prize, awarded by The Academy of American Poets; and *Music Minus One* was a 1996 National Book Critics Circle Award finalist. She received a fellowship from The John Simon Guggenheim Foundation, and was a Fellow in Poetry at The Mary Ingraham Bunting Institute (formerly The Radcliffe Institute), an Alfred Hodder Fellow at Princeton University, a Goodyear Fellow at The Foxcroft School in Middleburg, Virginia, and a Jenny McKean Moore Writer-in-Washington at The George Washington University in Washington, D.C. She has twice received grants from The National Endowment for the Arts.

Jane Shore was a Briggs-Copeland Lecturer on English at Harvard University, and was a Visiting Distinguished Poet at The University of Hawaii. Her poems have been published in numerous magazines, including *Poetry* (for which she received The Bess Hokin Award), *The New Republic*, *Ploughshares*, and *The Yale Review*. She is a professor at The George Washington University and lives in Washington, D.C., and in Vermont with her husband, the novelist Howard Norman, and their daughter, Emma.